20TH CENTURY
fashion

THE 80^s & 90^s

POWER DRESSING *to* SPORTSWEAR

For a free color catalog describing Gareth Stevens Publishing's list of high-quality books and multimedia programs, call 1-800-542-2595 (USA) or 1-800-461-9120 (Canada). Gareth Stevens Publishing's Fax: (414) 225-0377.

Library of Congress Cataloging-in-Publication Data available upon request from publisher. Fax: (414) 225-0377 for the attention of the Publishing Records Department.

ISBN 0-8368-2603-5

This North American edition first published in 2000 by
Gareth Stevens Publishing
1555 North RiverCenter Drive, Suite 201
Milwaukee, Wisconsin 53212 USA

Original edition © 1999 by David West Children's Books. First published in Great Britain in 1999 by Heinemann Library, Halley Court, Jordan Hill, Oxford OX2 8EJ, a division of Reed Educational and Professional Publishing Limited. This U.S. edition © 2000 by Gareth Stevens, Inc. Additional end matter © 2000 by Gareth Stevens, Inc.

Editor: Clare Oliver
Picture Research: Carlotta Cooper/Brooks Krikler Research
Consultant: Helen Reynolds

Gareth Stevens Series Editor: Dorothy L. Gibbs

Photo Credits:
Abbreviations: (t) top, (m) middle, (b) bottom, (l) left, (r) right

ICI: pages 28-29
Spreckley Pittham: pages 5(ml), 11(mr)
Redferns: Cover (br), pages 5(tr), 6(tr), 7(mr), 16(bl), 20(tr, bl), 21(t), 22(tr), 24-25, 25(br), 27(br)
Frank Spooner Pictures: pages 4(tl), 8(tr), 8-9, 9(tr, br), 10(tl, bl), 11(br), 13(tr, br), 14(tl), 15(br), 16(tl), 18(tl, ml, bl), 18-19, 19(tr), 22(br), 25(bl), 27(ml), 28(br), 29(tr)
© *Vogue*/Condé Nast Publications Ltd. / Michel Arnaud: Cover (tl), pages 3(tl), 5(br), 10(r), 11(ml), 12(r), 13(ml), 15(bl) / Alex Chatelain: pages 7(br), 14(tr), 15(tl) / Patrick Demarchelier: pages 14(b), 26(bl) / Arthur Elgort: Cover (bl), pages 6(bl), 7(tl), 22(bl), 22-23, 23(tr), 26(tr), 27(tr) / Robert Erdman: page 12(l) / Tim Geaney: page 23(br) / Michel Haddi: page 8(bl) / Kim Knott: Cover (tm, b2), pages 7(bl), 24(tl, br) / Steve Landis: page 17(bl) / P. Lange: page 17(r) / Peter Lindbergh: Cover (bm), page 29(bl) / Andrew Macpherson: Cover (mr), pages 3(mr), 6(br), 21(r) / Tom Munro: page 28(bl) / David Parfitt: pages 26-27 / Sudhir Pithwa: pages 4-5(b), 26(tl) / Albert Watson: page 16(m)

With special thanks to the Picture Library and Syndication Department at *Vogue* Magazine/Condé Nast Publications Ltd.

Printed in Mexico

1 2 3 4 5 6 7 8 9 04 03 02 01 00

20TH CENTURY

fashion

THE 80^s & 90^s

POWER DRESSING *to* SPORTSWEAR

Clare Lomas

Gareth Stevens Publishing
MILWAUKEE

Contents

For career women, power dressing meant projecting an image of businesslike glamour.

After stock markets crashed in October 1987, a softer, less aggressive look replaced power dressing.

The High-Tech 1980s and 1990s

The 1980s and 1990s were decades of rapid technological advances, including the Internet, CDs (compact discs), and satellite television. More than ever before, people were bombarded with information, and cultures and styles cross-fertilized.

Rave arrived late in the 1980s and gave fashion a new lease on life. This "clothing for clubbing" was not confined to the clubs for long.

Politics also had an enormous impact. Economies swung between recession and boom, causing social unrest as capitalism took hold and workers lost basic rights.

Since the 1950s, youth movements had influenced dress, but, in the 1980s and 1990s, twenty- and thirty-somethings took center stage. During the boom of the 1980s, yuppies bought into a lifestyle of designer suits and high-tech accessories. By the time stock markets crashed in 1987, however, yuppie power dressing had had its day. Greed was replaced by conscience, whether people raised money for AIDS victims or campaigned on environmental issues, such as the destruction of rain forests.

Mobile phones and digital organizers were fashion statements as well as business tools.

Designers such as Katharine Hamnett and companies such as The Body Shop turned fashions and beauty products into political statements. Supermodels became major celebrities, and designers, under pressure, raided every look, from current subcultures to fashions of the past.

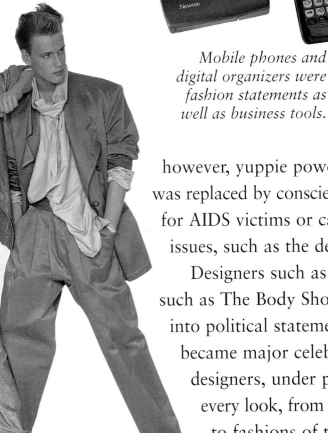

Jean-Paul Gaultier, with his sculpted bustiers and evening gowns, created a vogue for wearing underwear as outerwear.

Froth and Frills

In the early 1980s, unemployment was high, especially in Britain, which was experiencing its worst recession in fifty years.

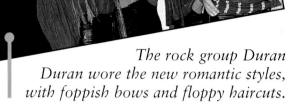

The rock group Duran Duran wore the new romantic styles, with foppish bows and floppy haircuts.

Rifat Ozbek created this punky version of the dandy look in 1987.

LONG, SHORT, OR SHORTER

This time of uncertainty was reflected in fashions. Three different skirt lengths could be worn: a gathered, three-quarter-length "peasant" skirt; a slightly shorter "pencil" skirt; or a flouncy, tiered "ra-ra" that ended at mid-thigh.

OLD-FASHIONED FRILLS

Romantic fashions were one way to escape the harsh economic problems of the time. Laura Ashley (1925–1985), famous during the 1970s for her loose-fitting, flowery dresses, advocated the romantic look. She used lace and old-fashioned techniques, such as broderie anglaise, pin-tucking, and smocking, to trim delicate pinafores worn over layered petticoats.

LAVISHED WITH LACE

Lace was central to the new romantic look, and velvet and brocade were used for knickers and vests. Colors were rich — deep maroons or forest greens — next to the bright, white lace shirts with ruffled collars.

Key to the new romantic look were extras, such as vests and cummerbunds. "Dandy" details included velvet lapels and ribbon-covered seams on trousers.

This romantic evening gown (1982) was designed by the Emanuels, who made Princess Diana's wedding dress.

In fact, ruffles were added everywhere, from necklines and cuffs to hems. Such frilliness also decorated the wedding dress of Lady Diana Spencer when she married Prince Charles of England in 1981. Diana wore a fantasy creation of ivory silk taffeta designed by husband-and-wife team David (*b*. 1953) and Elizabeth (*b*. 1953) Emanuel.

ROCK STAR DANDIES

Vivienne Westwood (*b*. 1941) also helped popularize the romantic look. Her 1981 Pirates collection was worn by rock stars such as Adam Ant, who dressed up in a gold-braided jacket and swashbuckling boots for his *Stand and Deliver* rock video.

BATTY GOTHS

In 1981, a new London club, the Batcave, became the birthplace of the goth movement. Recreating the gothic style of the 1800s, goths sought inspiration from novels such as *Dracula* (1897). Fabrics included velvet and lace, mixed with fishnet and leather, in black, blood reds, and purples.

Goth hair, dyed black, was backcombed to frame a somber face with severe black makeup accenting the eyes and lips.

BACK IN TIME

The romantic past, however, did not stop with pirates. Ralph Lauren (*b*. 1939) looked to the first settlers for his Prairie, or Frontier, collection. He used layers of striped and checked cotton fabrics, flannel shirts, hooded capes, and ruffled blouses for an American version of the nostalgic look.

A plume of ostrich feathers accents this lavish frock coat made of gilded silk brocade (1985).

New Man

As women became more independent, men began to lose their traditional role as breadwinner and head of the family. The family seemed to be in decline. The divorce rate soared, creating more single-parent families. Men needed to reinvent themselves, and the media was on hand to help.

CITY PATTERNS

From the beginning of the 1980s, men took a greater interest in looking good. The suit was standard city wear, but it was often jazzed up with showy accessories. Brightly colored vests and shirts were particularly popular. Designer Paul Smith (*b.* 1946), recognizing the new market and its spending power, launched his first menswear collection in 1976. He created shirts in bold prints of fruits and flowers for men confident enough to wear "feminine" patterns.

The new man was understanding, gentle, and sensitive. Some men were even called feminists.

This unbuttoned Moschino patchwork jacket (1988) reveals feminine rosettes on a rose-printed shirt.

MAKING UP

Cosmetics companies also were anxious to tap the new market of style-conscious males. Traditionally, men had used only aftershave, but, now, they were encouraged to buy facial balms, scrubs, and moisturizers. A company called The Body Shop pioneered a range of toiletries for men, and other companies followed close behind.

CARING AND SHARING

The media soon picked up on the new breed of feminized male and gave him the name "new man." A far cry from traditional, reserved males, new man was understanding and extremely sensitive. The most enduring image was Athena's poster of a bare-chested man holding a naked baby. When many men lost their jobs in the recession of the 1980s, some stayed at home to look after the children, while their female partners went off to work.

In the 1980s, briefs were definitely out, and boxers were in.

Jean-Paul Gaultier sent even men down the catwalk in skirts. Few — besides Gaultier himself — took up the style, but it certainly got plenty of attention!

MEDIA HYPE

Before long, new man experienced a backlash from some young men who resisted that image, preferring a rowdier, tough-guy look. Did new man or tough guy really exist? Both have been dismissed as media hype aimed at selling men more clothes, fashion accessories, and toiletries, and it cannot be denied that the 1990s saw an explosion of new magazines aimed at men. *GQ, Vogue Homme, FHM, Maxim,* and *Loaded* all sold in numbers large enough to suggest that men actually were interested in style.

BOOMING WITH BABIES

Babies attracted attention in the 1980s and 1990s, and the blockbuster movie *Three Men and a Baby* (1987) captured the mood. Tom Selleck, Steve Guttenberg, and Ted Danson starred as bachelors unexpectedly left to look after a baby girl. Whether or not new man existed, audiences enjoyed watching men cope in traditionally female roles. In real life, too, leaving nurturing only to women became outdated. Many magazines offered tips on forming equal relationships.

In addition to movie roles, Tom Cruise threw himself into the real-life role of father.

Power Dressing

During the 1980s, more and more women moved into high-powered jobs — and high-powered fashion. Power dressing for women was about being visibly successful in a man's world. In England, Prime Minister Margaret Thatcher wore smart, crisp suits.

Sue Ellen, wife of oilman J. R. Ewing in TV's "Dallas," had glamorous clothes and a super-rich lifestyle.

A WOMAN'S WORLD

Women in the workplace needed garments that were businesslike but elegant, such as tailored jackets with padded shoulders and suits in attention-seeking colors or pinstripes.

SOAP STYLE

Glamorous women who "had it all" were popular in prime-time television soap operas. These fashionable characters included Sue Ellen Ewing, played by Linda Gray, in "Dallas" and Alexis Carrington Colby, played by Joan Collins, and Krystle Carrington, played by Linda Evans, in "Dynasty." Television popularized a look for men, too. The stars of "Miami Vice" wore double-breasted designer suits with vests or T-shirts and Gucci loafers. Their designer stubble emphasized rugged masculinity — or were they too busy to shave?

"Miami Vice," with actors Don Johnson and Philip Michael Thomas, featured a casual look.

Top designers, such as Karl Lagerfeld at Chanel, Moschino, and Valentino, who designed this yellow ensemble in 1984, created expensive clothing for wealthy women.

SELLING A LIFESTYLE

Giorgio Armani (*b.* 1934) was the king of the power suit. He introduced diffusion lines — clothing with a designer label at an affordable price. He also created the power dresser's favorite fragrance, Giorgio, which was so popular it was banned from some restaurants! Other key lifestyle designers were Ralph Lauren (*b.* 1939) and Calvin Klein (*b.* 1942), and clothing stores, such as Next in Britain and The Gap in the United States, provided designer-style separates for "wanna-be" power dressers.

CRASHING

Many people, however, lost their glamorous lifestyles when stock markets around the world crashed in October 1987.

For the male executive, the ultimate in suit chic was an Armani, such as this one in Prince-of-Wales check.

Whether it was a Jaguar, a BMW, or a Porsche, the young professional wanted a car that was sleek, speedy, and expensive!

Glamour

While the suit was the essential daytime look for the corporate world, the evening belonged to ball gowns. Puffed sleeves and frills were extremely popular, along with sequins, lace, tulle, and taffeta.

HAVING A BALL

In 1986, a fashion by Christian Lacroix (*b.* 1951), called the puffball skirt, appeared on the catwalk. The skirt looked like a puffed-out ball of fabric. It was similar to Vivienne Westwood's "mini-crini," which was a shorter version of the crinoline dresses of the 1800s. Neither style caught on, but both captured the extravagant mood of the time.

GLITZY VERSACE

If money was no object, the most showy designer was Gianni Versace (1946–1997), who launched his first collection in 1978. Versace became famous for his use of extravagant fabrics and trimmings. He used mock animal prints, such as zebra, leopard, and crocodile, together with soft leathers encrusted with huge, faux jewels. Versace's enticing dresses launched the supermodels of the early 1990s.

A tight corset and a sculpted bolero emphasized the shape of the puffball skirt.

Never far from the headlines, Versace's designs made big news in 1994 when actress Elizabeth Hurley appeared at a film premiere in a black Versace dress held together with gold safety pins. Other celebrities who wore Gianni Versace included Madonna, The Artist Formerly Known As Prince, and Elton John, as well as Elizabeth Taylor and Diana, Princess of Wales.

Versace's design work for the theater and the ballet influenced his ever-dramatic fashions. This ball gown is from his Summer 1992 collection.

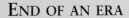

TOUCHES OF GLAMOUR

Although the House of Chanel underwent a makeover when Karl Lagerfeld (*b.* 1938) joined it, the classic quilted handbag with its "CC" logo and chunky gilt strap remained an essential for wealthy women. For those who were not so wealthy, fragrances such as Chanel's Coco for women and Egoïste for men provided designer glamour at a fraction of the price. Rolex watches and Cartier jewels accessorized ball gowns. Diamanté and faux pearl chokers were also popular — even tiaras made a comeback.

For men, a crumpled designer suit, such as this one by Girbaud (1984), was a casual, but expensive, alternative to black tie.

END OF AN ERA

The 1980s — at least for a lucky few — was a period of wealth. Capitalist economies allowed people to become successful with hard work. Money became easier to borrow. Some people took out large loans and made millions buying and selling stocks. For these people, however, misfortune struck. In October 1987, the stock market crashed, and the recession quickly spread. Real estate agents, for example, suffered when people failed to pay their mortgages, and housing prices fell.

Many investors lost fortunes when the stock market crashed.

The Japanese Look and New Age

Some people in the 1980s wanted more of an individual look than the power suit provided. They turned to the Japanese designers who first gained fame in the 1970s.

Issey Miyake opened Miyake Design Studio in Tokyo in 1970.

PLASTIC FANTASTIC

Japanese designers, including Issey Miyake (*b.* 1935), Rei Kawakubo (*b.* 1942) under the label Comme des Garçons, Yohji Yamamoto (*b.* 1943), Mitsuhiro Matsuda (*b.* 1934), and Kenzo (*b.* 1940), all placed enormous importance on texture. Miyake experimented with everything from woven bamboo to molded plastic. These designers layered, draped, and wrapped the body in fabric.

LIMITED PALETTE

To add emphasis to the texture, Japanese designers used a virtually monochromatic, or all in one color, palette, with odd dashes of a strong color, such as red.

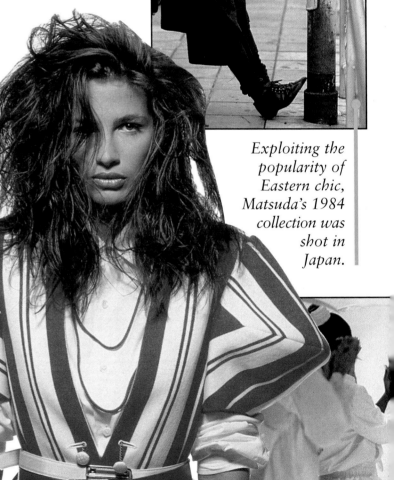

Exploiting the popularity of Eastern chic, Matsuda's 1984 collection was shot in Japan.

This Comme des Garçons jacket is from 1988, the year Rei Kawakubo declared that red was the "new black."

ANY COLOR, AS LONG AS IT'S WHITE

Western designers also came up with alternatives to power suits. Rifat Ozbek (*b*. 1953), for example, showed his new-age White collection in 1990. Although Ozbek's designs were influenced by nightclub wear, they expressed a desire to return to simple, clean living.

ECO-FRIENDLY FASHION

Ironically, environmentally unfriendly bleach was used to achieve Ozbek's pristine whites! From the mid-1980s, however, Katherine Hamnett (*b*. 1948) championed the "green" cause. Any truly eco-friendly fashion follower could wear her T-shirts made of cotton grown without pesticides. Often the T-shirts were printed with slogans for ecological or political concerns.

This Matsuda outfit in rough, cream-colored cotton has a buttoned sling that holds a matching blazer.

Rifat Ozbek took to the catwalk himself during a showing of his new-age whites. The key to his colorless collection was interesting textures.

SUPERMODELS

Despite a supermodel's astronomical fees, hiring one for a show almost guarantees front-page coverage in the international press. The amount of attention given by the press can make or break any designer's new collection.

Supermodels, such as Caprice Boulet (left), Naomi Campbell (center), and Claudia Schiffer (right), achieved international celebrity status. Some supermodels have even had look-alike dolls patterned after them.

The New Androgyny

Unisex, which had been an influential theme in the 1960s and 1970s, continued into the 1980s and 1990s. Unisex garments included jeans, sweatshirts, T-shirts, tracksuits, and leather jackets. Favored colors were black, gray, and khaki.

The star of Tank Girl, *a 1995 movie, dressed in androgynous army gear.*

GENDER BENDERS
As girls dressed up like boys, some boys dressed up like girls, including pop singer Boy George, who wore skirts and makeup. His long hair was sometimes braided and decorated with ribbons.

Boy George was the most famous gender bender of the 1980s.

WOMEN IN POWER
Even women's power suits, which used elements of masculine dress, could be seen as unisex. By the early 1990s, androgyny — appearing to be both masculine and feminine — was the fashion.

GIRLS WILL BE BOYS
Women plundered men's wardrobes for inspiration. Screen actresses, such as Marlene Dietrich and Katharine Hepburn, were already wearing trousers in the 1930s and 1940s. Since the pantsuits of the early 1990s were tailored to fit a woman's figure, they effectively retained her femininity.

In futuristic white makeup for lips, eyes, and hair, this model (1984) could be male or *female.*

TWENTY-FIRST-CENTURY GIRLS

Tank Girl, a comic-strip heroine residing in the post-apocalyptic twenty-first century, survived on her wits and streetwise resilience. In 1995, this cartoon was made into a feature film, starring Lori Petty and Malcolm McDowell. Tank Girl's clothes were distressed post-punk, with knee-high combat boots. She wore thick, protective gloves, torn jeans, and tight-fitting T-shirts. The overall effect, a look widely imitated by young women, communicated a refusal to obey the rules of traditional beauty.

MASCULINE MYSTIQUE

Jenny Shimuzu, who modeled in Versace's 1994 catwalk show, challenged stereotypes of beauty with her cropped hair and defined, muscular frame. Calvin Klein also picked up the theme when he launched two fragrances, CK One and CK Be, aimed at both men and women.

A WOMAN'S TOUCH

Female celebrities who have popularized a macho style include k.d. lang, Annie Lennox, Ellen DeGeneres, and Sandra Bernhardt. These women wear masculine-style clothing with plenty of attitude and confidence.

A tailored blazer and cuffed pants by Ralph Lauren suited the gender-bender look in 1984.

Even Chanel showed a man's-style tie with a double-breasted cardigan for women.

In 1979, Margaret Thatcher (b. 1925) became Britain's first woman prime minister. She held power for over eleven years.

Girl Power

Not until 1979 did Europe see its first ever female prime minister or president. Not surprising, then, that, during the 1980's, the independent woman became an important image in all media.

CHANGING VALUES

Women's magazines, such as *Cosmopolitan,* recognized that getting a man was no longer a woman's only goal in life. Women wanted careers and financial independence. A car advertisement, starring model Paula Hamilton, played on these new goals — a woman, in a show of independence, leaves her fiancé and drives off in a VW Golf.

STRONG WOMEN

For young women, pop stars were important role models. Strong, successful singer-songwriters, including Annie Lennox and Björk, were not afraid to defy convention. Lennox was known for her gender-bending suits, and Björk championed the cause of fresh young designers, such as Hussein Chalayan (*b.* 1970). Chalayan created beautiful evening wear out of Tyvek, a papery material that was previously used to make envelopes and protective coveralls.

In her 1990 "Blonde Ambition" tour, Madonna wore a satin corset with a reinforced bustier designed by Jean-Paul Gaultier. In 1996, as a mother, she chose a very different look.

MATERIAL SUCCESS

Madonna was, perhaps, the biggest pop success of all. Many people copied her constantly changing style. From the very beginning, she was unafraid to show her ambition — or her body. In the film *Desperately Seeking Susan*, she wore tight tube skirts rolled down to reveal her midriff. In the video for her hit single "Vogue," her outfit called to mind the slinky evening wear of 1940s Hollywood. Madonna was also famous for wearing Gaultier-designed underwear as outerwear.

LARA CROFT

Lara Croft, heroine of the Playstation game "Tomb Raider," ran, shot, swam, and skied — and looked good at the same time! She wore revealing, skintight clothing.

Lara Croft might be seen by some as the ideal woman of the 1990s, except she was not real.

SPICE ATTACK

Fans of the Spice Girls could pick and choose from five different styles — sportswear (Sporty), baby-doll dresses (Baby), animal prints (Scary), designer fashions (Posh), or slinky and daring (Ginger). The Spice Girls launched Girl Power in the mid-1990s, stressing that girls could be strong and outspoken. Their first hit single firmly stated, "I'll tell you what I want, what I really, really want!"

The Spice Girls (from left to right): Sporty, Baby, Scary, Posh, and Ginger (who left the band in 1998).

Subcultures

Music and dance influenced the way people dressed throughout the twentieth century. In the 1950s, teenage fans of rock 'n' roll copied their idols to the last button and zipper. In the 1980s and 1990s, music revolutionized and, again, influenced fashions of the time.

B-BOYS AND FLYGIRLS

When hip-hop and rap were born in the Bronx district of New York City, deejays created a new sound in music, providing some of the rhythm by "scratching" records on a turntable. B-boys, or break boys, showed off their break dancing skills to this new music. Although hip-hop started in the mid-1970s, it did not hit the mainstream until the 1980s. By then, girls had a nickname, too — flygirls. Both b-boys and flygirls wore designer sportswear, athletic shoes, and chunky gold jewelry. Some of the boys shaved their hair into stunning patterns.

DANCE MUSIC

After hip-hop, more new styles of music evolved. Techno developed in Detroit, house in Chicago, and rave came alive in London and Manchester, England. These unique new sounds were created by mixing together different pieces of music and sound effects. There was no longer a star on stage for fans to imitate, but fans were too busy dancing anyway.

Salt-N-Pepa's 1987 hit "Push It" was one of the first rap tunes to climb the pop charts. Fans of their music imitated the bright, baggy clothes worn by these flygirls.

Techno cyberpunks and bands such as The Prodigy wore industrial accessories and leather.

To rave meant to dance for hours without stopping. Cropped tops helped the dancers stay cool.

Although users of the drug ecstasy adopted the smiley face as a mascot, this drug kills!

DANGEROUS AND DEADLY

In the 1980s and 1990s, rave and dance music became associated with the illegal drug ecstasy. Although this drug made ravers want to dance all night, it was extremely dangerous. Users became dehydrated and sometimes died. Even worse, drug dealers began to make ecstasy with cheaper chemicals, such as rat poison, that could prove deadly.

RAVING ALL THE WAY

Rave had its own style, but athletic shoes were a must. Other elements borrowed from the b-boys were baggy jeans, T-shirts, and hooded sweatshirts. For girls, hot pants, cropped tops, or minidresses were the coolest clothes for dancing all night. Rave dancers accessorized with attention-getting hats, jewelry, and whistles — for joining in with the music.

Rave fashions borrowed from both the new and the old. This outfit is reminiscent of the colorful, swirling patterns popular in the 1960s.

Sportswear as Streetwear

Because athletic shoes, tracksuits, cycling shorts, and leggings were stretchy and comfortable, they were worn as casual clothing on the streets and in clubs. For people who could afford it, a designer label was essential!

STREET CREDIBILITY

Whether the latest in fashion was Nike, Adidas, or Reebok, logos and labels were important for street credibility. When the band New Kids on the Block wore Nike, fans followed the lead.

In 1986, hip-hop band Run DMC made the Top 10 with their single "My Adidas." Band members wore their Adidas unlaced.

Protective pads guarded against sports injuries.

SPORTS BOOM

The fitness fad started in the 1970s with roller skating and aerobics, and fitness clubs sprang up everywhere in the 1980s and 1990s. The new indoor fitness craze was step aerobics. Outdoor sports enthusiasts surfed, skateboarded, in-line skated, and snowboarded. Nike's advertising slogan "Just do it!" summed up the desire to go out and push the body to the limit.

Skateboarders wore long, baggy shorts and flat, rubber-soled shoes.

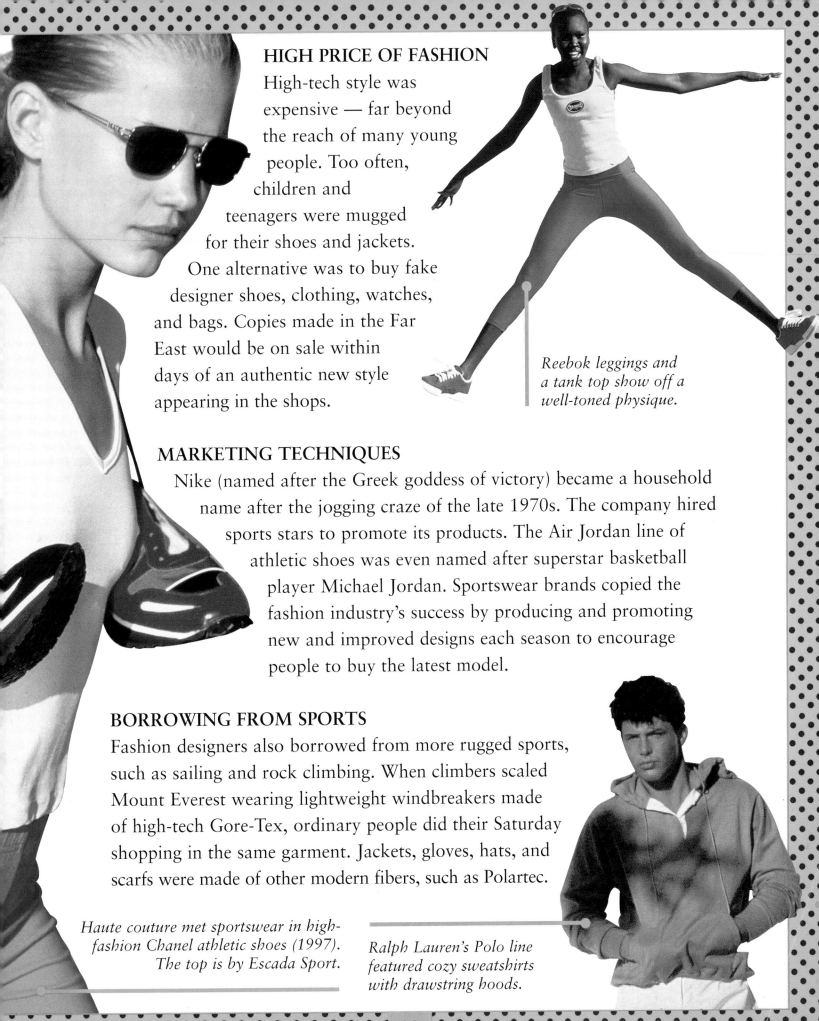

HIGH PRICE OF FASHION

High-tech style was expensive — far beyond the reach of many young people. Too often, children and teenagers were mugged for their shoes and jackets. One alternative was to buy fake designer shoes, clothing, watches, and bags. Copies made in the Far East would be on sale within days of an authentic new style appearing in the shops.

Reebok leggings and a tank top show off a well-toned physique.

MARKETING TECHNIQUES

Nike (named after the Greek goddess of victory) became a household name after the jogging craze of the late 1970s. The company hired sports stars to promote its products. The Air Jordan line of athletic shoes was even named after superstar basketball player Michael Jordan. Sportswear brands copied the fashion industry's success by producing and promoting new and improved designs each season to encourage people to buy the latest model.

BORROWING FROM SPORTS

Fashion designers also borrowed from more rugged sports, such as sailing and rock climbing. When climbers scaled Mount Everest wearing lightweight windbreakers made of high-tech Gore-Tex, ordinary people did their Saturday shopping in the same garment. Jackets, gloves, hats, and scarfs were made of other modern fibers, such as Polartec.

Haute couture met sportswear in high-fashion Chanel athletic shoes (1997). The top is by Escada Sport.

Ralph Lauren's Polo line featured cozy sweatshirts with drawstring hoods.

Grunge

In the early 1990s, the grunge look became popular, especially with students. This shabby, dirty, style was a reaction against fashion, particularly against the image of perfection projected by supermodels.

Grunge might consist of a brocade corset with garters holding up saggy cotton stockings.

ANTI-FASHION

In keeping with environmental issues of the time, the new generation of young people was concerned with recycling clothing and styles. They shunned high fashion by wearing recycled work clothes, such as jeans and flannel shirts, with combat boots or sturdy Doc Martens.

THE GRUNGE SOUND

When it came to music, the American pop band Nirvana, from Seattle, Washington, was as important to the grunge movement as the Sex Pistols had been to punk rock. Nirvana's multi-platinum album, *Nevermind*, included a track called "Sounds Like Teen Spirit."

Smashed eyeglasses completed this grungy John Galliano outfit (1985). Unrolled, the jacket sleeves hung down to the knees!

GRUNGE GURUS

Nirvana's lead singer, Kurt Cobain, and his wife, Courtney Love, from the band Hole, were key figures in the grunge movement. Love wore short, baby-doll dresses with big combat boots. Her bleached blonde hair was matted and showed dark roots. Dark lipstick highlighted her pale skin. Waiflike model Kate Moss, another grunge celebrity, found fame on the catwalk. She had pale skin, a gangly body, and lank, tangled hair. Along with looking bored, these features were ingredients for the grunge look.

The girl band All Saints took the grunge look into the mainstream. Band members wore combat-style pants, work boots, and anorak jackets.

DESIGNER GRUNGE

Many upcoming designers rebelled against slick couture. Belgian Martin Margiela (*b.* 1957) disregarded the usual catwalk venues and showed his collections in abandoned warehouses and train stations. He also used the lining of an outfit as a garment in itself, complete with unfinished seams and tailor tacks.

Displaying grunge layering, this New Yorker is wearing a shirt and a heavy vest, with a sweater around her waist. Her long skirt reaches the top of her hiking boots.

FATAL GLAMOUR

Drugs have contributed to the deaths of many celebrities. In 1993, actor River Phoenix died, at age twenty-three, after taking a lethal cocktail of heroin and cocaine. The movie industry has been blamed for glamorizing drugs in films such as *Pulp Fiction* (1994) and *Trainspotting* (1996), but some fashion designers could also be blamed. In the 1990s, some designers exploited a look called "heroin chic," using thin, pale models with dark, hollow eyes.

Kurt Cobain's use of dangerous drugs led to his suicide in 1994.

Retro Fashions

The final decades of the twentieth century saw many revivals of past styles. Every fashion seemed to be revisited for inspiration. John Galliano (*b.* 1960) exploded onto the fashion scene in 1984 with collections that drew on every possible past style, from frock coats to kilts to Dior's hourglass New Look.

Shoes and gloves by Chanel in 1987 saluted the 1960s.

In 1984, pop star Kid Creole stepped back into the 1940s in this woolen zoot suit.

BACK TO THE 1970s

With so many different images appearing in so many different media, no single look was considered "in." Individuality counted more than anything. One era, however, proved to be the most popular for borrowing — the 1970s.

FLARES WITH FLAIR

Just about every designer, from upcoming Alexander McQueen (*b.* 1969) to well-established Gucci, showed flares, hip-huggers, or pedal pushers in the 1990s. Shoe design also took a trip down memory lane as platform shoes made a comeback. When designer Vivienne Westwood used platform shoes in her famous 1993 collection, supermodel Naomi Campbell fell over in them! To add a modern twist, platform soles were added to 1990's athletic shoes, as worn by Baby Spice of the Spice Girls.

French designer Yves Saint Laurent revisited the 1960s in 1988 with this sequined shift.

BACK TO THE 1960s

From the 1960s, designers borrowed hot pants, ankle-length maxi-skirts, and caftans. Tight, ribbed T-shirts, polo shirts, halter tops, and tops with a keyhole neckline also came back. Many designers used 1960s-style stripes or psychedelic patterns.

These metallic flares and their coordinating silk jacket are by London's Workers for Freedom (1992).

BACK TO THE 1950s

The baby-doll look adopted by the grunge movement was based on night wear from the late 1950s. Baby-doll pajamas consisted of a frilly, feminine top with matching short pants. This look was picked up by designers Anna Sui (*b.* 1955) and Isaac Mizrahi (*b.* 1961) for their collections of 1994.

New-age travelers owed as much to punk style as to hippie fashions.

Labeled "new hippies" in 1988, when they appeared in Vogue, *this couple borrowed flower-power floppy velvet hats and ethnic beads.*

THE 1970s ARE BORN AGAIN

In the late 1990s, a revival of the musical *Saturday Night Fever* from the 1970s was a huge success on Broadway in New York City and in the West End of London. The 1970s were also highlighted in the movies *Boogie Nights* (1998), *Grease* (remastered in 1998), and a film version of the TV hit *The Brady Bunch* (1995).

Tribute band Bjorn Again played the music of ABBA.

The Technology of Fashion

Advances in the chemical industry during the 1980s and 1990s created a range of exciting new fabrics, and state-of-the-art computers controlled machines for designing them. Du Pont's wonder fabric Lycra was improved and joined by new synthetics, such as Tencel, Polartec, and Gore-Tex.

ALL-WEATHER FRIEND

Gore-Tex provided a waterproof, windproof, and breathable fabric suitable for outdoor sports, such as snowboarding. In 1998, Nike brought out Gore-Tex-coated running shoes. In autumn 1999, Ralph Lauren's brand-new label RLX introduced Gore-Tex in its ski, cross-training, snowboard, and cycling collections.

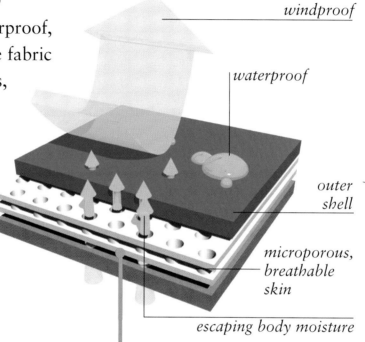

windproof

waterproof

outer shell

microporous, breathable skin

escaping body moisture

inner lining

Gore-Tex protects against the elements, yet allows perspiration to evaporate. It is the perfect fabric for outdoor sportswear.

Gore-Tex's waterproof "skin" contains billions of pores. Each pore is twenty thousand times smaller than a raindrop but seven hundred times bigger than a molecule of water vapor — such as perspiration.

As technologies improved, textile manufacturers were able to experiment by bonding different fibers. Here, natural silk is combined with synthetic nylon.

in the 1980s and 1990s

A computer controls the production line at this textile plant. Designers also use computers to design their new collections.

Picking up on the vogue for recycling, French designer Myrlold transformed plastic bags into fashionable and eco-friendly dresses and coats.

GOING "GREEN"

Environmental concerns led manufacturers to develop new, eco-friendly fabrics. Polartec, a thermal fleece, is made from recycled plastic bottles. Tencel, a strong, stretchy fabric, is made from renewable wood pulp. Tencel was used by designers Calvin Klein and Donna Karan in their collections.

SCI-FI FASHION

As the fashion industry moves into the twenty-first century, new technologies are providing even more amazing fabrics. Designers Deborah Milner and Errol Peak are already creating space-age metallic clothing made with polyester-coated stainless steel and aluminum yarns.

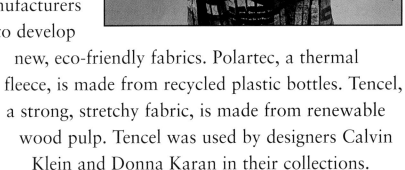

Natural rubber made a comeback in the 1980s and 1990s. This black rubber dress by Jean-Paul Gaultier is accessorized with a clear plastic belt.

· T I M E L I N E ·

	FASHION	WORLD EVENTS	TECHNOLOGY	FAMOUS PEOPLE	ART & MEDIA
1980		•Start of Iran-Iraq war •Poland: Solidarity movement	•Transformer toys hit the market	•John Lennon shot	•Anthony Burgess: Earthly Powers
1981	•Emporio Armani opens		•First space shuttle, Columbia, launched	•Prince Charles and Lady Diana marry	•The Face launched
1982	•Vivienne Westwood: "Savages" collection	•Falklands War: Britain defeats Argentina	•First artificial heart transplant	•Princess Grace of Monaco dies	•Ridley Scott: Blade Runner
1983	•Lagerfeld is design director at Chanel	•U.S. and Caribbean troops invade Grenada	•CDs first go on sale •AIDS virus isolated	•Lech Walesa awarded Nobel Peace Prize	•First episode of "Dynasty"
1984	• John Galliano: "Les Incroyables" show	•New Zealand declared a nuclear-free zone	•Apple Macintosh launched	•Bob Geldof sets up Band Aid pop charity	•Madonna: "Like a Virgin"
1985	•Karan: bodysuit •Levi's 501s relaunched	•USSR: Gorbachev becomes Communist Party secretary	•U.S.: Tele-shopping •Sinclair's 3-wheel C-5		•Norman Foster: Hong Kong and Shanghai Bank
1986	•Yamamoto: "Red and Black" collection	•Chernobyl nuclear disaster	•Space shuttle Challenger explodes	•Cory Aquino wins Philippines election	•Richard Rogers: Lloyds Building
1987	•Lacroix opens own couture house	•Stock markets crash		•Terry Waite taken hostage in Beirut	•Toni Morrison: Beloved
1988	•Bill Gibb dies	•End of Iran-Iraq war •Lockerbie air disaster	•Stephen Hawking: A Brief History of Time	•Pakistan: Bhutto named prime minister	
1989		•China: Tiananmen Square massacre	•Nintendo launches Game Boy	•Khomeini dies	•Chadwick: Enfleshings •Batman
1990	•Philip Treacy opens own hat business	•Gulf War breaks out as Iraq invades Kuwait	•Hubble Space Telescope launched	•Nelson Mandela freed in South Africa	•Philippe Starck: Juicy Salif lemon squeezer
1991		•Breakup of USSR •Yeltzin leads Russia	•Dyson's bagless vacuum cleaner wins design prize	•Aung San Suu Kyi wins Nobel Peace Prize	•Pat Barker: Regeneration
1992	•Patrick Cox: "Wannabe" loafers	•Australia drops oath of loyalty to Queen			•Frank Gehry: "Powerplay" armchair
1993	•Westwood's platforms trip Naomi Campbell	•PLO and Israel sign peace agreement		•U.S.: Bill Clinton elected president	•Stephen Spielberg: Jurassic Park
1994	•Hurley wears Versace's safety-pin dress	•South Africa: Mandela is first black president	•Channel Tunnel completed	•Kurt Cobain commits suicide	•Tarantino: Pulp Fiction
1995	•Jean Muir dies	•U.S.: terrorist bomb blast in Oklahoma City		•O. J. Simpson acquitted in murder trial	•Lori Petty: Tank Girl
1996	•Galliano at Dior • McQueen at Givenchy	•"Mad Cow" disease: bans on British beef	•Sony launches Playstation		•Walt Disney: Toy Story
1997	•Stella McCartney at Chloé •Versace shot		•IBM's Deep Blue beats Kasparov at chess	•Diana, Princess of Wales, dies	•Jurassic Park: The Lost World
1998			•Construction begins on International Space Station		
1999	•Errol Peak: aluminum wedding dress	•Serbians drive Albanians from Kosovo		•Madonna becomes face of Max Factor	•Star Wars: Episode 1 – The Phantom Menace

Glossary

androgynous: having both male and female characteristics; being neither obviously masculine or feminine.

brocade: a rich, silken fabric with raised designs woven into it, usually in gold and silver threads.

broderie anglaise: an embroidery technique that features patterns of cutwork, or holes, and stitching.

bustier: a tight-fitting, corset-style, strapless bra that extends to the waist and is worn both as underwear and outerwear.

capitalism: an economic system based on private or corporate ownership and the competitive distribution of goods and services in a free market.

dandy: a male who pays an excessive amount of attention to his personal appearance.

Doc Martens: heavy-duty leather shoes with a padded collar, laces, and thick rubber soles, designed in the 1940s as orthopedic-style footwear but adopted by skinheads and punk rockers in the 1960s and 1970s.

Gore-Tex: a waterproof and windproof synthetic fabric that "breathes," or allows the passage of air and perspiration through it.

Polartec: a fleecelike synthetic fabric with excellent thermal, or heat-retaining, properties, which is made from polyester and recycled plastic.

ra-ra skirt: a very short, usually frilly, skirt originally worn by American cheerleaders.

Tencel: an exceptionally strong, wrinkle- and shrink-resistant synthetic fabric made from wood pulp.

wanna-be: a person who tries to look or act like someone or something else to which he or she aspires.

yuppie: short for "young, upwardly-mobile professional;" an ambitious young man or woman pursuing a professional career.

More Books to Read

20th Century Fashion. John Peacock (Thames and Hudson)

The Dynamics of Fashion. Elaine Stone (Fairchild Publications)

The End of Fashion: The Mass Marketing of the Clothing Business. Teri Agins (William Morrow & Co.)

Fashion Sourcebooks: The 1980s. Fashion Sourcebooks (series). John Peacock (Thames and Hudson)

Fashion World (series). Miriam Moss (Crestwood House)

Fifty Years of Fashion: New Look to Now. Valerie Steele (Yale University Press)

Gianni Versace: Fashion's Last Emperor. Lowri Turner (Trans-Atlantic Publications)

Japanese Fashions. Ming Ju-Sun (Dover)

Secondhand Chic: Finding Fabulous Fashion at Consignment, Vintage, and Thrift Stores. Christa Weil (Pocket Books)

Surfers, Soulies, Skinheads, and Skaters: Subcultural Styles from the Forties to the Nineties. Amy De LA Haye (Overlook Press)

Web Sites

Fashion Icon. *www.fashion-icon.com/*

firstVIEW Collections Online. *www.firstview.com/designerlist/home.html*

Hemporium. *www.hemporium.co.za*

Gothic Fashion. *www.threethirteen.net/lace/fashion.html*

OnlineNewsHour extra. Fashion Issue. *www.pbs.org/newshour/on2/fashion.html*

Due to the dynamic nature of the Internet, some web sites stay current longer than others. To find additional web sites, use a reliable search engine with one or more of the following keywords: *designers, eco-friendly clothing, fashion, Gaultier, glamour, gothic fashion, grunge, Kenzo, latex, power dressing, rave, retro, rubber, sportswear, Tencel,* and *yuppies.*

Index